HOW TO HAVE AN HEALTHY AND HAPPIER RELATIONSHIP

BY

DR DOUGLAS CARLA

TABLE OF CONTENT

INTRODUCTION;

- The Secret to Having a Happy Marriage

Using this professional advice could lead to a happy ever after.

To start, even happy couples have disagreements.
As with any partnerships, there are ups and downs in every marriage.
Happy marriages, however, listen to each other's points of view, spot when an argument is veering off course, and intervene to correct it. Therefore, having occasional disagreements or going through a difficult time with your spouse does not necessarily indicate that your marriage is miserable. In fact, it's likely a sign that you're normal.

1.Utilize each other's advantages.

It's not always simple to look past tiny irritations, and there may even be occasions when you resent your partner.But in order to have a good marriage, you must be able to set reasonable expectations and accept your partner's skills and weaknesses. For instance, if you are better at math, try not to get upset when they balance the checkbook incorrectly. Make it your responsibility to set the budget instead. If cooking is their specialty, they can handle dinner preparation instead. "Daily use of our strengths is related with better well-being," Additionally, we feel higher relational satisfaction when we encourage our spouse to play to their strengths.

2.Don't look to your partner to make you whole.

It was very romantic, but in the real world, it wouldn't work.
It might result in an overly dependent relationship where neither of you are developing personally if you depend on your spouse to make you happy.

Healthy couples should instead "complement," not "complete," one another. "We should be open to the other person while being safe, mature, and entirely ourselves." So, rather than waiting on your partner to fill the hole, be sure to foster your own interests and wants by enrolling in a class you're interested in or making arrangements with friends.

But continue to work together. Together, enjoy yourself.

In order to maintain a happy marriage, it's essential to not completely rely on your spouse, but it's also critical to share mutual experiences. "Introducing new activities and interests into your relationship can enhance the bond.

3.When a couple pursues a special interest or develops a talent together, such as taking tennis lessons or culinary classes, they grow closer. "
Couples who are happy together are full of life. These experiences strengthen their relationship, whether it's through a shared love of travel, a strong desire to start a family, or a commitment to a cause.

4.Decide to be drawn to your spouse.

Whether you find your partner attractive is up to you. Yes, you can choose to remain attracted to your spouse throughout your marriage, despite what you might think. To achieve this, concentrate on the qualities that most appeal to you, such as your spouse's amazing legs or their parenting style (it need not be physical). The good news is that you can be attracted to someone even if they aren't a cover model. “The foundation of a happy marriage is a feeling of kinship. "Physical attraction goes much beyond appearances."

5.Join in the laughter.

Since life is difficult, it's helpful if you can find humor even when things are tough.

A couple's sense of humor usually indicates that they have different viewpoints. She claims that happy married couples seem more at ease with one another. She thinks that sharing laughs with your spouse, whether it be through small inside jokes, an unexpectedly amusing text, or even just binge-watching your favorite comedy, may strengthen your relationship.

6.Being understanding and respectful of your spouse is crucial. If you are critical and judgmental, it usually results in defensiveness and resentment. So, to maintain harmony in your marriage, refrain from criticizing your spouse's personality when you're angry. For instance, she advises against saying, "You're such a slob! Your dishwashing is never done. Try something like, "Because I made supper, I'd really love it if you could clean the dishes tonight," as an alternative. See how much more pleasant that sounds?

7.Celebrate the little victories. The majority of us are aware of how crucial it is to support our partners during trying times. She adds that it's equally crucial to remember the positive times as well. She claims that although happier events do occur more frequently than unhappy ones, couples frequently pass up these chances to get close. Therefore, tell yourself to stop what you are doing and give your partner's excellent news, like a compliment from their boss, your entire attention right away. Asking them questions and actively expressing joy at the wonderful news will help them enjoy the moment. By doing this, you'll express your thanks for your marriage's joyful times.

8.Respect one another.

It's simple to take someone for granted when you're around them all the time, so you should openly thank them every day. We all need to be recognized and reinforced for the things we are doing well, whether you're praising them for something kind they did or telling them something you enjoy about them. If your partner brings you coffee in the morning, for instance, tell them it made your day. "If we don't feel appreciated, we could get angry and distant from one another."

9.Accept change and prepare for it.

I really believe that in order to be truly happy in marriage, spouses must be prepared to change and adapt as our needs change, as do the people in our relationships.Therefore, what we require now might not be what we require in the future: "It's essential to bend, flex, and pivot with each other in a balanced dance. Because in a healthy marriage, one partner helps the other develop into their best selves, which calls for both individual and collective maturation. Up to the end of time.

CHAPTER 1;

- Things to Do Today to Make Your Relationship Healthier

Your relationship needs upkeep to ensure that both parties are content and content, regardless of how long you've been together and if you each have your own groove in the sofa or whether you just started dating while you were in quarantine (just ask these celebrities!). People asked relationship-focused therapists what couples can do, starting right now, today, to strengthen their bond and feel more affectionate almost immediately. Their advice is simpler than you might imagine!

1. Schedule leisure time

When you use humor, have fun together, and laugh throughout the day, it will strengthen your relationship. "The couple that plays together stays together." You can accomplish this in a variety of ways, such as by sending each other amusing GIFs through text, snuggling up on the couch to watch a stand-up special, or simply cracking up over a game of Twister.

2. Tighten ties

On happiness, physical touch can have a significant impact. This is especially true if you've been dating for a while and don't reach—literally!—for your partner as frequently as you did in the beginning, as that contact gives us a sense of connection and desire. It's acceptable to express your concerns and request space if you're a parent who feels overburdened by the prospect of increased touch because your children are with you constantly. Just make sure to let your partner know when you need it.

In light of this, greater physical contact may put pressure on couples to have sex when they may not be ready or in the mood for it. So stop talking about having sex. Like when you were dating, give each other a hug and kiss. "In relationships, human contact is crucial."

3. Foster a sense of teamwork

It's simpler to solve problems when you have a clear plan to find a solution that benefits everyone on your "team" from the start.

What is a choice you both could accept?

assuming that "we're in this together, and we'll get out of it together" is the best way to approach situations. Stop letting selfishness destroy your relationship.

4. Keep in mind your relationship goals

When your partner enters the room and does something you don't like right away, take a moment to regroup. "Consider the thought, 'Wait a minute. Will jumping on them move me closer to achieving my aim of having a pleasant night or further away? You can concentrate on what you're doing to ensure that your marriage is happy if you keep in mind what you want it to be. Other than getting angry, you can manage anything your partner does.

5. Be willing to believe them.

Don't assume your partner won't comprehend your point of view if there is a misunderstanding. “When we give them the benefit of the doubt and engage with them about their viewpoint, that helps resolve any issues swiftly. Assuming the worst is self-protective.

6. Simple ways to channel date night

"Extract the essence of desire," I say. Even if you're unable to go out on dates right now, try to recall what made those early times of "dating" so special. Invoking those memories and making the other person feel loved and cared for by saying things like "I just want to tell you: I love you" or "I find you adorable" brings back those memories.

7. Be frank when discussing the future.

"When people reveal their goals and dreams, they feel incredibly exposed." Letting your partner know about your ambitions, whether they are personal or professional, "may help you feel closer." Giving each other the chance to encourage personal growth can foster mutual respect, however keeping your goals to yourself could lead to animosity if one of you starts to alter unexpectedly. Growing and changing throughout time is "very beneficial," especially if you can do it together.

8. Work on listening empathically.

It's so simple to use your catch-up time to compare notes on who had a rougher day. But first, show your partner some compassion before adding your stress to their day's venting.

9. Change things up

A relationship benefits much from novelty in order to remain strong and successful. "Creating new rituals prevents you from being stagnant. Try taking an online course together, hiking somewhere you've never been, or just spending time in a park as a couple. Something new causes the release of stimulating, gratifying neurotransmitters.

Give yourself permission to let the kids watch more screen time if you don't have childcare so you can go out and do something as a family (even if you're watching on a shared iPad with shared headphones while the kids use the big TV). This is hardly the moment to be concerned about excessive electronic use. If the pair is healthy,

10. Decide on a second chance

When your partner did (or didn't) something, did you snap at them? Make a repeat request. You can tell them, "I don't like myself when I'm not empathetic," and pause to consider your desired behavior as opposed to your previous response. Retry after that. You won't believe the difference it makes! If you give it some more thought and you're still angry that they didn't hang their towel back up, just the act of taking the effort to express your complaint in a more sympathetic manner will lessen antagonism.

11. Avoid criticism and instead be constructive

Prepare a reassuring foundation for your main points before commencing a meaningful conversation.Be careful not to express your dislike for the person. Always frame it in terms of what you would adore. To clean the dishes tonight, for instance, rather than saying, "You never clear the table, it's your turn," would make me pleased. This works because you're "thinking about what you need and what you desire, then putting it in a positive way," rather than "thinking about their drawbacks."

12.Create a "love" list.

Tell your partner three qualities you value and enjoy about them at the conclusion of the day. Even the smallest gestures, such as "you refilled my coffee" or "you filled up the gas tank," will go a long way toward preventing any potential animosity. “People who feel resentful frequently only want to feel acknowledged. One of the first constructive, proactive things you can do for a relationship is an act of concern and forethought that is followed by a sincere thank you.

13. Present modest gifts

Don't automatically assume that every gift needs to be carefully considered and expensive. These can be lovely for special occasions, but more often tiny acts of kindness, like flowers (even ones gathered from your yard!), a kind word on a Post-It note, or a favorite sandwich, can keep couples close. These tiny trinkets act as a constant reminder of how well we know our partners, that we were thinking of them, and how much we genuinely value them.

14. Press the hold key.

Don't become upset if a serious topic of conversation is met with diversion or resistance. Choose a certain time to bring up the subject again. This is crucial if one person wants to speak it out while the other wants to get some sleep. Say, "We'll discuss it Saturday morning." The one who wants to talk it out is given a deadline, while the person who wants to sleep is expected to keep their promise to ultimately discuss it.

15. Give yourself some time.

Even though it might seem counterintuitive, putting more emphasis on your relationship can benefit from self-care. "We're not accepting responsibility for our own happiness if we want our partner to make us happy." Make time for activities that "fill your cup" and make you happy, and you'll find that your mood is less influenced by what your partner does or doesn't do. (Ask them for assistance with this, too. If you have children, ask your spouse to watch them for a few hours so you can make the most of your limited free time.) 'Your partner can be the icing, but you have to be your own cake,' is a saying I like to use.

CHAPTER 2

- The 10 Truths of Happy Relationships

Here are the requirements for creating a strong relationship.

If your relationship isn't happy, how can I make it so? Be aware that successful partnerships aren't just a matter of luck. To desire to be together, both parties must put in constant effort and dedication.

A link thrives when there is a "happy relationship." It's the shared objective you both share for the future of your partnership.

Many factors are similar to healthy partnerships in general. An extended, fulfilling relationship can be maintained by being aware of these "truths."

What constitutes the basis for relationship happiness?
I concur that communication and trust are the cornerstones of a strong foundation.

The facts of happy couples
My experience working with patients has led me to the conclusion that harmony, open communication, love, and respect are key components of a happy relationship.

"Happily married couples occasionally quarrel, but they never lose sight of their fundamental regard for one another.

Here are some other characteristics of fulfilling relationships.

1. Continue to view committed relationships realistically

You won't experience butterflies in the stomach forever. Every relationship experiences ups and downs, as said. Realistically, nothing will be all sunshine and flowers.

Maintaining a realistic perspective enables you to cherish each minute spent with one another and fosters your relationship even through trying times.

2.Maintaining a relationship's "tone" entails paying close attention to it and giving it frequent attention, just as you would a living thing.

It can be compared to "resistance" training. Couples can enhance their relationship fitness over time by working through difficulties and obstacles together.

3. Frequently hang out together
You need to spend time with each other on a regular basis for relationships to mature and thrive.
A relationship needs quality time because it fosters the emotional (and frequently physical) connection.

Spending time together is crucial in long-distance relationships.

"If you have ways to feel connected even though you don't spend much time together, it can be okay if you reside in separate cities or someone travels frequently for work.

In order to create enduring memories, couples should make time in their schedules for quality time.

4. Frequently relish independence

A healthy relationship might also include time apart from one other. Different couples have various demands for independence. There is no issue as long as both partners are content with the balance of interdependence and autonomy.

A relationship might be nurtured by novelty-infused time apart, or it can just feel lonely.

Each pair must openly address this and ensure that the proper balance is struck.

5. Respect each other's uniqueness
Being with people that are unlike you can be beneficial to your relationship.

Try to consider any benefits that might come from your partner's differences.

Encourage yourself to consider it a benefit, at least occasionally.

6. Don't expect (or attempt to force) a partner to change "You can communicate how you feel, but you

can't force your partner to change. You are the only person you can alter.

A conscious decision to change on their own will be made by your partner with the aid of effective communication.

"A person who is passionate about fitness and health can't make their partner share the same enthusiasm, but their persistence and drive to lead a better lifestyle can definitely inspire their relationship.

7.Pick your battles.

In a committed, healthy relationship, conflict is sometimes inevitable. But it's also critical to acknowledge that not all battles can be won.

Consider the question, "Will this matter in 10 years?" Let it go if the response is no. Simply said, worrying about petty issues is not worth it.

8. Know how to communicate and listen effectively.
All relationships depend on communication, thus if you can't express yourself clearly to your spouse, your voice won't be heard.

9. Cherish honesty "Honesty is actually the foundation of intimacy [To] feel deeply connected with someone, you can't lie or withhold information."

When discussing honesty, one person said, "When our partner understands us and all of our shortcomings, it helps us feel more sincerely loved."

10. Displaying respect for each partner in public
Daily showing your partner respect demonstrates to them your worth as a partner and your ability to be trusted.

"An excellent method to demonstrate outward displays of respect is to take your partner's thoughts and opinions into consideration and make concessions for them.

CHAPTER 3

- What are signs of a happy relationship?

Partners in a healthy relationship are those who:

1.Respond to "healing attempts" after arguments and don't take themselves too seriously (can laugh at themselves).

2.When discussing their partnership, each prefers to use "we" rather than "I."

According to our specialists, there are a few more characteristics of happy partnerships that you might observe. Various partners:

3.Actively considers and takes actions that they know will make the other happy and doesn't openly criticize the other's decisions shows compromise.

Benefits of being in a healthy relationship for mental health

4.You can greatly improve your quality of life and improve your mental health by having strong, healthy connections through:

5.Enhancing your general mental health and self-confidence

6.Supplying internal relationship support lessens the signs of anxiety and despair

7.Expanding empathy

8.Growing hope and optimism in romantic relationships

It takes work and dedication to have a happy, healthy relationship, as well as a shared desire to want to be with your partner. According to psychologists, communication and trust are the cornerstones of a great relationship.

Relationship specialists concur that happy partnerships share a number of characteristics. Happy couples put in the effort, from spending quality time together to choosing their battles.

A few indications of a great relationship include feeling emotionally supported and safe. Your mental health can also benefit from having a solid foundation.

A therapist can provide you with advice on what might be helpful if you are concerned about your relationship. If your relationship is having problems, think about talking to a qualified specialist.

CHAPTER 4

- Ways to Keep Your Relationship Happy And Healthy

Ways to Maintain a Happy and Healthy Relationship

Relationships are difficult, but happy couples are able to handle the ups and downs and weather the storm. Learn from the pros with these ten suggestions for maintaining a happy and healthy relationship. (And sure, you ought to engage in sexual activity daily!)

1. Be open with others
According to research, communication style plays a bigger role in determining whether couples will remain happy than

commitment levels, personality qualities, or stress. Healthy relationships know how to maintain open lines of communication even when there is difficulty. The best conversations between happy couples take place without the interruption of phones, tablets, and laptops.

2. Keep in Mind the Little Things

Please and thank you should not only be used in business settings. Even while dating someone for 20 years, manners are crucial. Treat your spouse with the same respect that you would show a visitor. Make nice conversation, use the words "please" and "thank you," and why not give your partner a drink? A mutually respectful environment can be maintained with just a few polite gestures.

3. Workout collectively

According to studies, couples who workout together are not only healthier but also happier in their relationships. According to many studies cited by Psychology Today, the signs of physiological arousal—the high you get from working out—mimic the consequences of sexual and romantic excitement.

4. Take a Vacation

Both traveling alone and going on a couple's retreat can revitalize a relationship! Many contented, healthy couples go on quick getaways together or travel frequently together. It can be quite powerful to be by yourself, make new acquaintances, or go on adventures without your partner. In the end, you'll come home to your lover feeling inspired, motivated, and more in love than ever.

5. Laugh

Laughter releases endorphins, calms the entire body, and strengthens the immune system .Smiling and laughing, even when it's forced, will make you feel better. So, even if you and your loved one are having a difficult day together, try smiling and laughing just for fun. You will get happier and healthier just by laughing.

6. Share a meal.

Families who eat dinner together tend to stay together. The dinner table is a place where families and couples can interact and get spiritual and bodily nourishment.

Along with promoting optimal family nutrition, eating meals together at the table creates a regular, hallowed setting for interaction and entertainment.

7.Get intimate every day.

Having sex every day eliminates the anxiety some couples feel when it's time to "perform." Having sex can also improve your sleep, reduce stress, and possibly ward off prostate cancer! Partners who engage in daily sex claim that it strengthens their relationship and improves their physical health.

8. Sometimes switch roles

If it is both, the relationship could become monotonous and uninspiring. If he always drives, why not alter things up the following week and let her drive? Or, since she's always cooking, why not offer a few of his creations? Altering roles can provide some diversity and perhaps even open your eyes to your partner's perspective. It should go without saying that switching up roles in bed can liven up a relationship. If your partner usually initiates conversation, perhaps it's time for you to do so.

9. Accept physical change with patience.

As you age together, you will both change and mature. Because you have become so comfortable with one another, you might be quick to criticize each other's shortcomings. However, if you want your happy relationship to endure, you should never bring up your bald spot, beer belly, or stretch marks! The response to "How do I look?" is always "You look wonderful (and I love you)," no matter how old and wrinkled you both get.

- Ways to Fall In Love All Over Again

Bring back the passion from the early days of your relationship with these expert tips.

There are lots of great things about being in a long-term relationship: Research shows that happy couples, in many ways, have better health and overall well being than their single or divorced peers. After all, a loving partner can offer companionship, comfort, and physical and emotional support when you need it.

But after years of marriage or dating, a significant other can start to feel more like a roommate than a romantic partner. Maybe you've grown apart, you're busy with work and kids, or the spark's just not there anymore. For whatever reason you've found yourself falling out of love, here's how the experts suggest you find your way back in.

01
of 20
Be More Touchy-Feely

"Long-term couples don't touch enough. "When we touch—especially skin-to-skin—we get a little rush of the brain chemicals that help trigger those loving feelings." Think about how often you and your partner actually share physical contact on a daily basis. If it's just a quick peck on the lips before and after work, make an effort to step up your game. "Most married couples hug for three seconds or less. "So I advise them, two to three times a day, to stop what they're doing and hold a long, calm embrace. It can change your biochemistry, and you'll begin to bond again."

02
of 20
Sleep Closer Together

That same rush of brain chemicals can also come from physical contact in bed—and not just during sex, either. Sleeping skin-to-skin, whether it's full-on spooning or even just touching toes, can have relationship benefits, too. In fact, a 2014 survey presented at the Edinburgh International Science Festival found that couples who slept the closest to each other reported having more relationship satisfaction. "Of course we don't know if sleeping apart causes dissatisfaction or if happier couples simply sleep closer, but why not just try to get closer and see if it helps?. "Get the toddler or the dog out of the bed and try snuggling for at least a few minutes."

03
of 20
Limit Technology

"If you haven't put your family and your relationship on a technology diet yet, this is the year to do it. "Nothing is killing communication faster right now than guys staring at their iPhones while girls are trying to talk to them at the dinner table, or vice versa. "Otherwise, you won't give each other your full attention, and it's easy to become annoyed or feel disconnected."

04
of 20
Take A Vacation

If work and family obligations have forced you and your partner to put your love life on the back burner, schedule some time off from your regular responsibilities. Getting away may help you focus on each other (instead of distractions like the bathroom that needs repairs), but even a staycation or a long weekend at home—if you treat it right—can be enough to refresh your bond. Before you go, though, have an honest conversation about your expectations."It's important to discuss how much time you'll spend together, whether you want to have more sex than usual, and what you hope to accomplish in terms of your relationship. "It can feel unromantic to lay it out ahead of time, but it will reduce your chances of feeling disappointed if you both have different goals in mind."

05
of 20
Say Thank You

When you fall into habits in a relationship, you may take for granted the nice things your partner routinely does for you. And even if you do notice them, do you let him or her know you're thankful? Gratitude is important. "Put a note in his briefcase letting him know you appreciate that he gets the dry cleaning every week, "or touch her on the arm and thank her for bringing you Starbucks every day."

I suggest keeping a gratitude journal, and writing down three things every day you're thankful for—whether it's related to your relationship or not. "It can foster a sense of wellbeing and openness that can improve your connection with your partner."

06
of 20
Pucker Up

Locking lips can play an important role in the quality of a long-term relationship, according to a 2013 study from Oxford University. In fact, researchers found that frequent kissing was even more important to relationship satisfaction than frequent sex. "A 30-second kiss gives us a warm, fuzzy, safe bonding feeling from that cuddle hormone, oxytocin. "Partners can give this feeling to each other by practicing a hug and a kiss—a mini connection—in the morning before work and before bed at night."

07
of 20
Compliment Each Other

When you've been in a relationship for a long time, it's easy to focus on the negative,—which can lead to nagging, hurt feelings, and dissatisfaction on both sides. Instead try to focus more on the good things and less on the bad. "To use a garden analogy, water what you want to grow; don't water the weeds." Letting your partner know what you love about them—whether it's physical, intellectual, or emotional—can actually help you see him or her in a more positive light. "When I have couples in therapy who are growing apart, I make sure they start our time together by sharing some compliments back and forth."

08
of 20
Incorporate Surprise

To relive the feeling of falling in love.Weil, you've got to find new ways to trigger that rush of feel-good dopamine and oxytocin—like by incorporating novelty, excitement, and surprise into your not-so-new-anymore relationship. You may try "kidnapping" each other,taking turns on different weekends to plan secret activity or destinations. Or try something simpler: "Date night but with something new—a new restaurant, or even new food at the same restaurant."A weekend overnight in a new place, or a vacation without children; anything with the element of surprise."

09
of 20
Cultivate Your Own Interests

Falling in love with someone isn't all about what happens when you're together; a lot of it has to do with what you're doing on your own. "People become passive in their relationships when they become disengaged, and one of the main reasons they become disengaged is because they're not satisfied with their own lives." That's why she encourages clients to make sure their lives contain something they feel passionate about individually—something their partner doesn't necessarily share. "Say you love horseback riding. "If you come home from a ride feeling energetic and alive, you can bring a fuller, more engaged self to your relationship, as well.

10
of 20
Observe Your Partner's Passions

Likewise, it's important for your partner to have a passion, as well. And if you want to remember why you fell in love in the first place, find a way to witness your loved one in his or her most passionate state. "I have a friend who's married to a fisherman, and while she'll never share his love for fishing, she's happy to navigate his boat and just honor his talent and watch him in his element. "She gets to see him being alive and excited, and that's really the best way to see your partner."

11
of 20
Create Something Together

Once you've got your individual passions figured out, it's also helpful to have something you can both pour your love and attention into. "The couples who last the longest tend to be the ones who create something together

Often that something is children, but it can also be a business, a charity, or even a home-remodeling project. "Look for something you are both interested in—not just something you're into and you think your spouse can get on board with. "When you work together on something you care about, you can see your partner in a different light."

12
of 20
Go On Double Dates

You don't need to spend all of your time one-on-one. In fact, inviting friends along once and a while can help you and your partner reaffirm your love for each other. In a 2014

Wayne State University study, people who went on double dates with other couples they were close with said they felt more affection and romantic feelings toward their partners. It turns out that watching your other half interact with friends can help you remember what you love about him or her, say the study authors—and praising each other in front of other people (bragging about her new promotion, or telling stories about what a good cook he is) can be a turn-on for both of you, too.

13
of 20
Stare Into Each Other's Eyes

Any two people could fall in love by asking each other a series of 36 questions, then staring into each other's eyes for four minutes. "I've skied steep slopes and hung from a rock face by a short length of rope, but staring into someone's eyes for four silent minutes was one of the more thrilling and terrifying experiences of my life.

14
of 20
Flirt With Each Other

Staying happy in a long-term relationship requires balancing two basic needs."We crave security and knowing somebody's got our backs no matter what, but we also crave excitement and novelty and mystery. "The challenge is trying to have both of those things met by the same person—and one way couples can do that is by flirting with each other like they've just met."

Flirting can be different for every couple, but anything affectionate, sexually suggestive, or playful can fit the bill. And while it may feel awkward to send an inappropriate text to the person you've been married to for years, it can help add excitement to a romance that feels stalled. "The key is finding a way to do it so you both feel comfortable and you're having fun."

15
of 20
Work Out Together

Breaking a sweat with your sweetie may increase your physical attraction, as well as your emotional bond. Research has found that after being physically active together, couples reported more relationship satisfaction and being more in love with their partners—and that physical arousal (elevated heart rate, heavy breathing, etc.) can often elicit romantic attraction.

16
of 20
Engage In Pillow Talk

Research found that couples who disclosed positive feelings to each other after sex reported more relationship satisfaction than those who didn't. This may be part of the way committed couples maintain their closeness and their romantic bond, the researchers say.

For an even better relationship boost, spend a few extra minutes after sex chatting and snuggling. Couples who engaged in post-sex affection (such as cuddling and caressing) were generally happier with their sex lives and relationships overall, even three months later. "The findings suggest that the period after sex is a critical time for promoting satisfaction in intimate bonds,.

17
of 20
Don't Play Games

If you're feeling distant from your partner, you may think that putting on a sexy dress or doubling up on your sessions in the weight-room is the best way to get his or her attention and jump-start your flagging romance. And that may work—but it could also backfire: "If he or she doesn't read your mind or notice that you're trying to impress him or her, you could end up feeling worse and resentful. Instead, sit down to talk honestly about how you feel. "Say something like, 'I don't feel particularly connected to you right now, and I have some thoughts about what I'd like to do differently to make us feel closer. "That way, it's less of a test that your partner passes or fails—you're in it together, and you're both making an effort.

18
of 20
Redefine Date Night

Scheduling regular time to be by yourselves as a couple, away from your work and home responsibilities, can help you stay connected and remember what you love about each other. But that doesn't have to mean getting all dressed up and going out to a fancy dinner—it can be as simple as taking a walk together every night and discussing your day. "Going on a date can be the time you look at your partner not as a co-parent or a co-homeowner, but as the person you built your life with. But couples should decide what's romantic to them.

19
of 20
Be There For Each Other

Contrary to popular belief, it is possible to be in a long-term relationship and maintain feelings of romantic love (and not just comfortable companionship) for many years. One secret to this lasting attraction? Having your partner's back, and knowing that your partner also has yours. Adults who feel secure in their relationships tend to have higher self-esteem, the study found, which correlates to more feelings of "intense, exclusive focus" on their partners. "Thus, having the felt security that a partner is 'there for you,' not only makes for a smooth functioning relationship, but also may facilitate feelings of romantic love," the authors wrote.

20
of 20
Adjust Your Expectations

Even with all of these tips, no relationship will be perfect—and that's the most important thing to remember if you're feeling dissatisfied with your love life. "We live in such a sexualized culture, people come in thinking something's missing if they're not having 50 Shades of Grey sex and swinging from the chandeliers. Before you decide your romance isn't good enough, remember that all long-term unions have ups and downs, and that love can be felt and expressed in many different ways. "A lot of people end up in therapy because their expectations don't match the reality of their life, and they're hoping to change their environment."Sometimes, what they really need to change is their outlook."

CHAPTER 5

- Simple Ways to Make Your Boyfriend Happy

Making Your Boyfriend Happy: How to Do It

Not just girls need to be content in a relationship for it to be successful. Naturally, your partner needs the incredible joy you can bring him as well. In a relationship, it's crucial to make your partner happy. In actuality, that is one of the elements that will help your relationship grow and last.

Now, if you're having trouble thinking of ways to cheer up your guy, you've come to the proper place. To learn more, see the list below.

1. Congratulate him.
Boys enjoy receiving compliments just as much as girls do. Who wouldn't appreciate hearing that they have beautiful looks or are intelligent? The myth that men don't care about their appearance is no longer true. Tell your sweetheart what you admire about him, what drives you wild about him, or how handsome he looks in that white shirt. He'll undoubtedly smile as a result of it.

2. Tell and demonstrate your love for him.
It's not difficult to express your affection for him, and it's not even more difficult to demonstrate your adoration for him. Say "I love you" or take other small steps to show your affection, like letting him go.

3. Relieve him.

Be there to soothe him when he's worn out from work or school or if he's been going through a lot lately. His dreary days can be made brighter with a simple embrace, kiss, or words of encouragement like "You'll feel better," which would also highlight the contours of his lip.

4. Pay attention to him.

It's not always a good idea to take your guy for granted. Instead, focus entirely on him and create a sense of desire for him. Put down the phone and pay attention while he speaks. Every minute you spend with him is incredibly essential, so give him the respect he deserves.

5. Be truthful with him.

One of the finest ways to make your guy happy is to be honest, no matter how challenging it may be. Always be honest with him and don't hold anything back. In such a scenario, not only will you make him happy, but you'll also experience the same sense of fulfillment he does since he'll be sincere with you.

6. Give him some room.

One of the most crucial factors in making your lover happy is this. You probably enjoy spending time with your partner, but every relationship has times when you both need to have space to develop as individuals. Give him room to be alone, to hang out with friends, or to concentrate at work.

7. Rely on him.

If a person doesn't feel trustworthy in a relationship, they won't be content. Simply by giving him space, encouraging kindness, sharing your feelings, having confidence in your partner's talents, and letting him use his phone alone, you may demonstrate your trust in him.

8. Be supportive of him.

One of the crucial things you should do to keep him content is to have the desire and capacity to be a supportive partner. Be his cheerleader, encourage him in his work and hobbies, pay him compliments to make him feel good, and respect his aspirations for a profession. Your help will be valued.

9. Be a lively female.

Be impulsive and upbeat when you're with your guy. Attempt to make him smile or find something enjoyable to do together. Together, you can try a brand-new sport or visit a new location. Just keep in mind that the goal is to have fun here rather than spend money.

10. Hug him.

When it comes to tender affectionate moments, guys are like butter and they like gentle embraces. So, unexpectedly approach him and give him a bear hug; he will admire you for it.

11. Help him feel valued.

Making your partner feel appreciated on a regular basis is a terrific method to make him happy. Take note of the little details on him, such as his new haircut. You can also prepare a meal for him, bring him coffee, or express your love and devotion to him. These small gestures will undoubtedly help him become happier.

12. Shock him.
Even though it seems straightforward, doing this is one of the finest methods to keep your partner content. It needn't be a big or expensive gift because what matters is the thought. You can bake for him, take him out, pack him a lunch, bring him breakfast in bed, write a love letter, or even give him a massage.

13. Be there for him constantly.
Be there for him when he needs a shoulder to cry on or is feeling sad. If you stick by his side to comfort him throughout his dejected mood,

it would mean so much to him. You just need to listen and be there; you don't need to talk much. You are more than enough to make him happy just by being there.

14. Embrace his faults.
Everyone has imperfections to cope with, but having someone who can accept them makes it easier. Accept that your lover is imperfect, concentrate on what makes your mate special, and watch as the good grows.

15. Authenticity.
Who would be content with a mate who is a master pretender? Of course, we all desire a partner who is secure in her own skin. Instead of pretending to be someone else, just be yourself and continue to look lovely. The easiest thing you can do

to make your husband pleased is to do that.

16. Smile.

A guy can't help but smile when he sees his girl pleased. Therefore, try to smile, laugh, and be happy whenever you are around him because your happiness is also his delight.

- How to Make Your Boyfriend Happy Over the Phone

1. Wish him a good morning
first thing when you talk to him. Say something like, "Good morning, honey. I love you." Just let him know that you are available for him all the time, no matter what else is going on in your life at that particular moment.

2. Talk about the good experience you've had together.
Remember your most recent trip together? Talk about the different tourist attractions you saw. Then, share with him all the fun, interesting, and unique experiences that you had there.

You want to remind him of the wonderful memories you shared together. That way, you constantly remind him that you are a great girlfriend producing wonderful memories together.

3. Listen carefully when he is talking.

Show him that you are interested in what he has to say, no matter how boring it may be. Avoid interrupting or being distracted by anything else that might be going on around you at the moment.

Your boyfriend wants to see that his opinion matters to you so that you are willing to listen patiently.

Show interest in what he has to say by asking questions about the topic.

It shows that you are actually listening and trying to have a decent conversation with him.

Make sure your boyfriend knows that his feelings are more important than anything, including your own personal interest.

4. Don't interrupt while your boyfriend is talking to you on the phone.
Interrupting a conversation is not only disrespectful, but it's hurtful for the relationship because it shows that the person talking doesn't matter much at all to you.

When he is talking, give a short response, such as "ok", "hm" to let him know you are listening.

If you are given a chance to respond, do not go off the topic.

It will mess up the conversation and make him feel more uncomfortable.

Let him complete what he wants to say without being distracted by anything else going on around you or in your life at that moment.

If he pauses after saying something, don't fill the silence by jumping back into the conversation. Wait until he's done talking before you talk. Let him know that his opinion matters a lot to you and the outcome of what he had to say is important.

5. Compliment him.
Complimenting means letting your boyfriend know that he is special to

you. But you don't need to overpraise him.

For example, compliment him on how he looks, how well he is doing at his job or school, etc.

If you can't find anything to compliment, just let him know that he makes you happy all the time, even when he is only talking with you through the phone. Tell him, "I'm so happy talking with you."

He will feel very loved when he hears such words from you, no matter how simple they may seem to be.

It is very important that your boyfriend knows how much you value his friendship and love. Make sure he knows exactly what it is about him that makes him special to you.

6. He is free to talk about anything with you.
Tell him that you are there to listen whenever he wants to talk, no matter what it is about.

Do not judge him about what he will tell you or try to convince him why he should feel a certain way.

Show him that he can talk openly with you about any topic, no matter how serious or trivial it might be. Make sure you have no hidden agenda while talking to your boyfriend about anything.

7. Talk with your boyfriend as often as possible.

Spending time together in person is one of the best ways to let the relationship grow stronger, but it may not be possible all the time, and that's where phone calls come in.

If you can't go out with your boyfriend, call him up on the telephone.

You don't have to spend hours talking on the phone, but make sure you do talk at least a few minutes once a day so that your boyfriend knows that he is still important to you. Talking often will help keep him interested in you.

Try to set up a specific time every day to talk on the phone. Make it a habit and try not to miss it.

8. Always have a positive attitude while talking to your boyfriend on the phone.
Make sure he knows you are always there for him, even if you are not always pleased with what he does.

Stay supportive and encouraging when you talk to your boyfriend on the phone. It would help if you let your boyfriend know that you care about his feelings and opinions, but at the same time be firm enough to make it clear that there must be mutual respect between both of you.

9. Be gentle and flirtatious while talking to him on the phone.
If your boyfriend knows that he can make you feel good just by talking, he'll be more likely to call you more often in the future.

You should do some things that will let him know how much you like talking with him. Showing how much his love means to you will make your conversations more special, fun, and romantic.

10. Be yourself when talking on the phone with your boyfriend.
Always be yourself and show him that you are the same person both in person and on the phone. If he is always around you, he should know how to expect you to talk on the phone.

11. Put down all distractions.
So that you can fully concentrate with him without any interruptions or concerns.

Calling your boyfriend may not be a big deal for both of you compared to meeting each other in person, but it still requires some attention from both of you. You should never ignore your boyfriend when he calls because this will make him feel disregarded and ignored since now isn't really a good time for him.

Please make sure you are both on the same page so that your boyfriend will never be distracted and confused about what to do during his calls with you.

12. Make sure he can feel your warmth when you talk.
When talking on the phone, both of you should be able to sense that you are both genuinely happy and excited about spending time with each other, no matter how much distance is between you.

You should never sound as if you don't want to talk or appear distracted when he calls. Always make your tone sound as if there is nothing else except being together with him. Listen attentively while he talks and respond appropriately by giving your full attention without letting anything distract you from him.

CHAPTER 6

- How to Make Your Boyfriend Happy Over Text

1. Send him a brief but heartfelt good morning text.

Sending your lover a sweet good morning text is the quickest and easiest way to make him smile over text.

Although it may seem stupid, it is the ideal place to begin. Here, keeping things brief, straightforward, and sweet is crucial. You might be up before him every day, so why not make his morning by sending him a short good morning text? Here's an illustration:

"I just wanted to let you know that you're on my mind! I hope you have a wonderful day.

2Point out all the adorable and humorous things that your guy does.
It will reassure him that you know how to make him smile both in person and over text. If he consistently does something cute, mention it occasionally both verbally and in messages, just as you would in person.

When those behaviors recur in front of your boyfriend, flaunt them anytime they do so by saying that they make you grin.

3. Remind your boyfriend of your love for him.

It's simple to develop a messaging routine with your lover and start taking him for granted. Texting him messages with love quotes or ones that express your feelings is a terrific method to show him that you still care.

You can tell your lover how happy you are in person or via words on a screen. This will show him that even when he doesn't perform well in other areas, he can still make his lady feel safe and cherished.

"You hold a very special place in my heart." Additionally, "I love being with you!"

4. Highlight his accomplishments or the things that bring him joy.

It's safe to assume that if you've been dating for any length of time, you both have accomplishments or interests that the other doesn't mind at all. Here is an example: You can tell your lover how happy you are in person or via words on a screen. This will show him that despite his flaws in other areas, he is still capable of making his lady feel loved.

"I'm proud of you for working so hard! I know how much that meant to you."

5. Sing him your favorite song, of course.
A quick and easy technique to cheer up your partner and get him ready for you to sing the song he likes is to sing a cheery little tune to him over text. Obviously, if it makes him happy, this behavior can become

commonplace for both of you, and that's okay!

He can be having a rough day, but when you tell him about this, it instantly makes him feel better. If done properly, it can be adorable!

6. Express your misses for him.
He'll appreciate the reminder of how much you adore being with him, even if it appears ridiculous, and that you seize every opportunity to be with him. Here's an illustration:

I'm eagerly anticipating the weekend. I long for a chance to cuddle with you.

7. Discuss a line from a book or movie you both enjoy.

What are some uplifting lines from books or movies? This is a cute, simple way to let your lover know that, even if he might not be physically present, you still value the occasion just as much as if he were.

8. Reminisce about great times you had together in the past.
Additionally, this will make your lover giggle and serve as a reminder of how much fun you two used to have. Here's an illustration:

Do you recall the time we got lost in the woods? It was enjoyable.

9. Only positive information about oneself should be shared.
Perhaps you recently completed a task at work or have great plans for the next weekend. The statement "I

did really well during my presentation today" is sufficient. Alternatively, "I had a great time tonight; I'm delighted we went out!"

10. Simply say "I love you."

One of the simplest and most straightforward methods to express someone's value is to do this. Their day will be made a thousand times better just by you telling them how much you value them! Here's an illustration:

I haven't told you yet, but I adore being with you today.

11. Just be truthful about how you're feeling.

Being open and honest with one another about your feelings is a terrific way to demonstrate your connection even when you are not in the same room with your boyfriend, even though he should already know most of the time or have some concept of what's going on in your head and heart by this point.

12. If he doesn't reply right away, don't SMS or lose your cool.
Recognize that he might be busy or there may be other people around. Just be patient and wait for his response; he'll make an effort to get back to you as quickly as possible.

- How to Treat Your Boyfriend Nicely

1. Prepare his preferred food.

2. Act as his biggest supporter.

3. Address him affectionately.

4. Enjoy some quality time with him and his family.

5. Send him brief notes.

6. Be sure to complement him.

7. Give him many lengthy embraces.

8. Create a unique present for him.

9. Always stand by his side.

10. Remind him daily that you love him.

- How to Get Your Man to Smile

1. Have a lot of happiness.

2.Give him the reins.

3. Quit being a pest.

4. Honor him.

5. Show fidelity and loyalty.

6. Treat your hubby nicely.

7. Pardon him.

8. Refrain from letting pride into your heart.

9. Act as a good wife.

10. Act as a good mother.

11. Show your spouse's in-laws love.

12. Have self-love.

CHAPTER 7

- ### How to Keep Your Boyfriend Happy in a Relationship

Here are 25 pointers to help you if you want to know how to have a happy life with your boyfriend.

Love yourself as much as you love your mate.

Only when you and your partner are both content in your relationship can you truly be content. In order to make your significant other happy, you should love them as much as you love yourself. Always keep in mind that relationships are partnerships. Love and happiness must therefore be experienced and shared by both of you, not just one of you.

2. Possess reasonable expectations.

"Unrealistic expectations can be harmful because they make us and other people vulnerable to failure. Therefore, don't let your exaggerated hopes hinder you. Always keep in mind that relationships are partnerships. Love and happiness must therefore be experienced and shared by both of you, not just one of you.

2. Possess reasonable expectations.
"Unrealistic expectations can be harmful because they make us and other people vulnerable to failure. Therefore, don't let your exaggerated hopes hinder you. Keep in mind that your perspective on life affects your reality.

3. Have open conversations.
You can handle conflicts and avoid possible issues in your relationship

with open hearts and healthy communication. Additionally, you have the power to make your life—and the lives of those around you—more sincere and joyful.

4. Laugh.
Laugh heartily with your beloved someone. Your immune system will be boosted, your mood will improve, and you will be protected.

5. Take a trip with your significant other.
Take a quick getaway together and go on experiences to make your relationship happier and more passionate.

6. Share a meal.
When was the last time that the two of you shared a meal? Even though sharing a meal together is a little

gesture, it fosters intimacy, is a wonderful opportunity for insightful conversation, and increases enjoyment in your relationship.

7. Take a break together.
Play your preferred video game, take a trip, or go on a movie date. This will deepen your connection and help you become closer and more open with one another.

8. Be truthful.
You gain a tremendous deal of assurance and comfort from being honest. It benefits both of you.

9. esteem for one another.
Respect makes people feel valued and accepted, regardless of how different they are from other people, which in turn makes them

happier. Learn to respect your partner's judgments, opinions, and worldviews regardless of how dissimilar they are from your own.

10. Be positive.

Optimism is one of the essential factors for happiness. It can make a bad situation better and provide optimism during difficult times.

11. Discover forgiveness.

You can learn to forgive, and once you do, you'll experience peace of mind and joy in your heart. Keeping old baggage from someone who has harmed you around won't help you keep that balance in your life, so keep that in mind.

12. Avoid reacting angrily.

You may occasionally lose your composure and become enraged.

Additionally, you run the risk of escalating the situation when you react poorly to someone who is already agitated. Better to keep silent and wait for calmer conditions before speaking.

13. Express love.
Hugs, kisses, and tiny surprises are all appropriate ways to show each other the attention you both deserve. You'll achieve happiness and fulfillment in life in this manner because you'll understand that you are loved.

14. Make considerate gestures.
"You have the worst kind of heart problems if you don't have any charity in your heart.

Encourage individuals to practice kindness as a regular part of their lives so that they might try to inspire others.

15. Develop it.

To maintain a relationship functioning properly, you must invest effort into it. This implies that you must put up more effort by displaying affection, being kind, or performing any other deeds that will demonstrate your love.

16.Listen.

Achieving effective communication requires more than just talking; it also requires listening and undistracted attention to what is being said and done.

17. Pay attention.

Being aware of other people's beliefs, understanding your partner's needs, and your own understanding of the world around you are all necessary for happiness.

18. Encourage one another's passions.

Being in a relationship with someone who will support your life goals is wonderful. When a couple supports one another's interests, it enhances their sense of love and satisfaction in their relationship.

19. Make plans.

Moving in the direction of what you desire as a couple can also make you happy. Set goals, achieve them, and maintain a solid relationship.

20. Honor one another's accomplishments.

"Which man is the happiest? Whoever respects others' qualities and finds satisfaction in their happiness as though it was his own.

When the other person is genuinely delighted for you after hearing about your success, that is what makes a relationship cheery.

21.Fix the issue.

Never let a situation go unattended; instead, schedule a time to address it before matters worsen.

22. Honor each other's personal space.

You are not required to confine yourselves to each other's arms. Additionally, you need a little room for yourself, your pals, or your business. To live a healthy and happy life, take the time to respect one another's space.

23. Treat each other well.
The ideal relationship is one in which both partners adore, cherish, and spoil one another.

24. Workout with a partner.
Regular exercise is beneficial for the body and heart. Additionally, it makes you happier, especially if you exercise with a significant other. Not only will it make you feel more energised, self-assured, and also makes you happy.

25.Be ready to make sacrifices.
You have to give up some things if you want to be happy. True self-sacrifice entails being prepared to give up personal pleasures in order to improve, strengthen, and prolong your relationship.

- How to cheer up your boyfriend when he's down

1. Smile

2. Listen intently.

3. Invest time with yourself

4. Show them your appreciation

5. Offer some inspiration

6. Crack a joke or amusing story.

7. Express gratitude.

8. Give presents

9.Say "I love you"

10. Just to check on them, call or text.

11. Assist by offering guidance

12. Remind them that they are not alone

- Making Your Long Distance Boyfriend Happy: Some Tips

1. Express your emotions.

2. Repeated assurances.

3. Transmit handwritten poetry.

4. Ensure that you get together at least once a year.

5. Allow personal space.

6. Always be there for one another.

7. Don't go on and on.

8. Try your boyfriend's interests out.

9. You'll never run out of topics for conversation.

10. It's important to communicate.

CHAPTER 8

- Other ways to make him pleased

One word of advice

Even if these suggestions will improve your relationship, never go above and above to make your man happy until he reciprocates in kind. Ignoring this will lead to catastrophe!

Never, ever be overly kind and generous to someone who merely takes. That is how takers prosper and cause givers to lose hope in the possibility of a fulfilling relationship. It's admirable that you want to find ways to make your lover content. However, we sincerely hope he is also doing the same for you.

Let's move on from this word of warning and focus on the good aspects by looking at the greatest methods for making your partner happy. These are effective, and as soon as you use even a couple of them, your partner will begin to think of himself as the luckiest man alive!

Use these tried-and-true methods to make your man happy and lucky all at once if you want to know how to make your boyfriend happy every day in simple ways that can help him recognize how precious and amazing you are!

1. What drew him to you in the first place?

Improve that. Find ways to show him more of your best features, whether they are your hair, smile, or flawless figure, so he will never forget how amazing you are.

2. Support him in living his life

Men act masculine, but occasionally their personal lives are a disaster as well. Talking about his dreams will inspire him and assist him in achieving his objectives.

3Engage in sentimental acts

Nothing can make you feel more unique than an unexpectedly kind act.

4. Avoid making him feel uneasy.

Guys detest having insecurities. And rather than admitting or accepting that they are uneasy, they will become irritable or start to avoid you. It's a male issue. The less insecure you make a guy feel, the more he will adore you.

5. Make sure he doesn't take you for granted.
Taking someone for granted and feeling insecure are diametrically opposed. He'll start to take you for granted if he starts to feel too confident. To avoid boring him, try not to be too accommodating to him.

6. Request his aid.
Ask for his assistance when you need it. He'll feel better about himself and respect you more if you ask for his assistance in the appropriate manner.

7. Give him a bear hug just because.
When it comes to nice affectionate moments, guys are like butter. He

might not always ask for a hug, but he will appreciate the way you feel in his arms if you suddenly run up to him and give him a close embrace.

8. Use your PDA.
Most men don't care about displays of affection in public. But they adore it when their attractive partner holds onto their arm or gives them a public kiss on the cheek.

9.Inform him of any other guys you meet.
You might occasionally run into a bunch of guys. However, whenever you can, tell him about the guys you meet. If he is familiar with the other guy, he will feel more at ease and secure if they ever cross paths.

10. Put him first whenever possible.

When there are other guys around, don't ignore him. One of the most important things to keep in mind if you want to keep your partner content is this. He will respect you more if you make him feel like YOUR guy.

11. Tell him you believe in him.
Tell your guy you believe in him and that you do. A man becomes more devoted to his woman and exerts greater effort to maintain her happiness when he is aware that she trusts him.

12. Be open to trying new things in bed
Guys adore a woman who can act erratically in bed. However, you really don't need to bother with something if you're not prepared for it. He'll accept that you're not ready

if he loves you. Additionally, there are a ton of options to explore!

13.Tease your boyfriend, please.
Never give in too quickly. You'll be monotonous. Make him work for you in exchange for any sex room favors. He will respect and regard you more highly as a result, which is important in a romantic relationship.

14. Give him some room
Learn to respect your boyfriend's space if you want to make him happy. Men need to take breaks every day to spend time alone.

15. Be there for him to lean on
When he is down, lift his chin for him. Instead than pointing out his error, assist him in overcoming it. Everybody experiences horrible

days occasionally. And on those days, all your partner would want to do is fall into your arms and let the weight of the world's troubles melt away. Be there for him during such times, offer comfort, and reassure him that you don't think less of him for being vulnerable with you.

16. Don't drag out a conflict
Relationship fights and disputes can wear you both out and leave you both feeling sad and miserable. Any disputes should be resolved as quickly as possible.

17. Dress well for him
Guys are drawn to attractive girls right away. The same applies to your partner. When you're with him, dress nicely and look stunning, and you'll brighten his day.

18. Dress attractively in bed
If you two are in a close relationship, take care of your appearance in bed by dressing nicely. His goofy grin will always be there.

19 Get along with his family and friends
While boys have closer relationships with their own friends, girls spend a lot of time with their girlfriends. Make an effort to get along with his favorite buddies so that they would like you for the nice and approachable person you are.

20. When necessary, act like a guy.
Your guy may want you to be girly and feminine, but he would adore a woman who can tie her hair up and act like a man when necessary.

21. Give him praise

Men enjoy being complimented. Be sincere when you tell him what you appreciate about his mind and body. He'll never forget it.

22Make him feel valued.

Keep in mind his significant days and tasks, and let him know in advance. Do something kind for him without any prompting, like make him a beautiful supper or get him a stylish t-shirt.

23.Don't disparage him in front of others.

Men have enormous egos, yet they are also quite vulnerable. The first thing he'll do is go into the arms of another girl who treats him better if you consistently put him down in front of others or disrespect him.

24. Land a solid blow.

Okay, so we're not arguing that blowing him off is the only thing that matters. If you don't like helping others, screw it, literally. Men want their girlfriends who are confident and talented in bed. You can play it cool everywhere else, but in bed, show him what you can truly do and how filthy and dirty you are.

25. Develop your dirty talk

Yes, dirty chatting is helpful, as awkward as it could be for a beginner. Then how! It can make every dirty meeting different and new, keeping your romantic life intriguing for years to come.

Your lovemaking abilities will hook a guy so hard that he won't want to be in bed with anybody else when combined with some dirty chatting.

26.Be a fun-loving girl.

Take a positive outlook on things and try to find humor in everything. Be impulsive and upbeat.

27. Keep yourself in check

Though it may come off as cruel and petty, we're being sincere. According to numerous studies, people begin putting on weight as soon as they enter a committed relationship. Don't belong to that group. Maintaining good health and physical fitness are important. not only for himself, but also for your own assurance and self-worth. Of course, it works both ways, so if your lover wants to continue to be attractive to you, he should also be maintaining his own attractiveness.

28.Don't keep secrets.

Guys like their girlfriends to be talented and bold in bed. You can be coy everywhere else, but in bed, show off your moves and let him know how dirty and naughty you can really be.

Especially those that can jeopardize the relationship or make him wonder about your motives. Of course, you are under no obligation to inform him of the information that you and your female friends have in good faith exchanged. However, let him know if there is something that can jeopardize your relationship.

29. Keep codependency at bay

The worst kind of codependency is! The fact that you two are always joined at the hip may cause you to initially feel like soulmates and completely in love. But very quickly, this intimacy could lead to relationship problems and drive you away.

30. Respect limits.

Healthy limits exist between healthy relationships. Of course, you could do both—share everything and spend every waking moment in each other's arms. However, if you want to keep your guy happy, you must learn to set healthy boundaries. Allow your lover to enjoy his own hobbies, just as you do. Additionally, be careful not to offend him or do anything that you know he doesn't like.

31. Jointly develop long-term plans

Making long-term plans together is a terrific approach to encourage your partner to work for a larger goal as a pair while also making him feel secure.

32. Assist him in achieving his life objectives

Do you know what your lover wants out of life? Has he got one? Talk to him about this, and encourage and support him in achieving them. Learn to be both your boyfriend's biggest supporter and his biggest critic if you want to know how to make your guy happy. If you can be honest with him and express your opinions to him, he'll respect you and them.

33.Don't give someone the silent treatment

This is despised by both men and women alike. If you remain mute in response to his abuse of you, that constitutes an act of emotional abuse. Instead, speak up and describe your feelings. Because of it, he will respect you more.

34. Take his advice.

You may believe you already practice this, but are you really? In the partnership, does he feel heard? Or are you checking social media as he talks about a problem he's having? Give your partner your full attention when he wants to chat to you. He will notice that you are paying attention and, more importantly, that you care.

35. Keep your feminine vigor.

Don't lose your femininity since it is part of what makes you YOU. Let him witness how full of beauty and feminine energy you are by jumping for excitement, laughing at the stupidest things, and swaying your hips during an impromptu dance.

36. Direct him and give him advice

Do you believe that he spends much too much time playing video games? Has he started to develop bad habits? Inform him that he is headed in the wrong direction by donning the boss pants. He might find this annoying and think you're being critical and dictatorial. However, if you communicate with him in a way that he can understand, he will be appreciative that you are in his life.

37. Speak with him

Please, speak honestly. When you have one of those leisurely evenings, sit down, put your phone aside, and just talk to him. What interests him? What is his goal? What is he dreaming of? Everything! Your man could act like a shell at times.

38. Touching him

These days, we're all touch-starved, and skin hunger exists, despite the fact that we may not be aware of it. When you lie on his chest, rub his shoulders and chest with your hands frequently. Cinch his fingers when you're seated next to him. The more you touch him, the more appreciative he will be of your love in his life.

39. Give him modest but thoughtful presents

Even though it's not much, we all appreciate the gesture. Buy your guy a gift that you know he'll appreciate and needs if you want to make him happy. Do you shop for food? purchasing clothing online? You can always find something for him to enjoy.

40. Avoid contrasting him with other men.
This final piece of advice is essential if you want to know how to make your guy happy and you must never, ever disregard it. Never, ever put your boyfriend in a negative comparison with another guy. In whatever small manner, telling him his friend is a better man than he is is the same as betraying him and crushing his heart! You might believe that what you're saying will help him become a better man. But he'll see it as you telling him the other guy is superior and he's not good enough for you. So please refrain from doing this. Ever!

There you have it—all the finest methods to make your partner feel fortunate beyond belief. Start implementing a few of these suggestions right away, and before you know it, you'll be holding a very content boyfriend in your arms.

When you use this advice on how to make your lover happy, he'll be beaming broadly every time he sees you. The best thing is that it will also demonstrate to him how exceptional and amazing you really are!

CHAPTER 9

- Does your partner ever have a change of heart?

Does it make you nuts, too? Here are some solutions if your boyfriend is unsure of himself.

It's been said that love and relationships are like jobs in that they change frequently until you find the proper one that keeps you there for the long haul. What happens if the right person is unsure of you? A guy who is unsure of himself is constantly shifting, "on the fence," and unsteady on his feet.

Will a man like this ever make a firm decision and keep his ground?

Or, even worse, will he ever meet the proper woman—the one who will persuade him to stick with it through the long haul? Or will he carry on making choices?

In fact, the term "indecisive" refers to the absence of a distinct and obvious conclusion. It is the inability to choose wisely when faced with multiple options: a momentary paralysis.

What causes someone to be unsure? People who lack clarity can be annoying. You are likely wondering why exactly your lover is unsure of himself. Here are a few typical explanations for why people struggle to decide.

1. Overanalyzing

Some folks simply think too much all the time. They simply consider all of their alternatives before being overly analytical. They are attempting to analyze the advantages and disadvantages of each option because they believe there are too many options.

Overthinking might eventually paralyze a person since there is People lose focus on the crucial elements of the judgments they must make when this occurs.

Realistically, individuals just have to acknowledge that it's occasionally difficult to predict every result. To put it another way, nobody can foresee the future. Therefore, it would be better if they admitted that some things were beyond their control.

2.Perfectionism

Some people are unable to make decisions until everything is ideal. But perfection is unattainable. What is ideal for you may not be ideal for someone else.

But other people simply won't do anything unless they feel that everything is "perfect" in their eyes. They can't bear the idea of things not going as planned or making blunders.

Additionally, they have a concept of "right" and "wrong." They also consider everything logically in order to select the best course of action. They fail to realize that any choice will have pros and cons for them. They are unaware that there is no such thing as a "perfect" decision.

3. Appealing to others

Some individuals struggle with decision-making because they are people-pleasers. Making decisions is a constant challenge in partnerships. Even simply a simple "What do you want for dinner?" or "What do you want to do today?"

If someone is having trouble deciding, it can be because they are overthinking what you want or emphasizing your wants too much.

Because you want to avoid upsetting your partner, you think they want to eat at that particular establishment. But you must also be sincere about what you desire. As you can see, some people find it difficult to decide since they are aware of another person's desire but lack the motivation to fulfill it.

4. Fear

Insecurity and fear go hand in hand. And insecure people abound in the world. Fear of the future and the consequences of our decisions is a common emotion.

They may also come to realize that they are scared of owning up to their actions. After all, no one likes to be held accountable for the negative consequences of their actions.

Additionally, they have a concept of "right" and "wrong." They also consider everything logically in order to select the best course of action. They fail to realize that any choice will have pros and cons for them. They are unaware that there is no such thing as a "perfect" decision.

5.Programming starting in early life
Some people's beliefs, personalities, and decision-making skills from their parents might still have an impact on them even if they are adults. It's possible that someone never learned how to make their own decisions because their parents were overbearing or controlling when they were young.

If this is the case, the person would be so preoccupied with worrying about how their parents would view their choices that they wouldn't know where to start. Additionally, if a person's parents were equally indecisive, they may have unintentionally adopted that trait themselves.

Someone can become unable to act and paralyzed by the fear of disappointing their parents. Even though they logically understand that it doesn't matter, they don't on an emotional and subconscious level.

6.Doubting oneself

Most people occasionally have self-doubt. And for certain people, these uncertainties can significantly affect their capacity for making decisions.

They doubt themselves even when they are certain of their choices or what is best for them because they lack confidence.

As a result, individuals can put off taking action because they believe their decision-making abilities are limited. For some people, insecurity may be crushing. As a result, their ambivalence might persist until they start to feel better about themselves.

7. Aversion to change

No matter how big or small the decision, our lives will change as a result of it. But change is always inevitable. It is an unavoidable fact of life. But some individuals simply dislike change.

CHAPTER 10;

- Things To Do To Make Your Girlfriend Happy

1. Send Her a Message in the Morning

Send your girlfriend a sweet good morning text message if you want to brighten her morning. You might just wish her a good morning or write her a sweet note expressing your gratitude for having her in your life.

2. Cite one of her favorite poems, books, or films.

Everyone has a favorite poem, book, or movie that they find reassuring. Discover the songs that your lady enjoys the most, then quote some of them. Your lady will appreciate your kind gesture and feel at ease and content.

3. Prepare her preferred breakfast.
When her significant other prepares meals for her, women are thrilled. And if it's her favorite breakfast, she'll be over the moon. The most significant meal of the day is frequently breakfast, so having her favorite breakfast prepared by her favorite person will make her day.

4. Send Flowers to Her
Various flowers have various meanings. Giving your girlfriend a variety of flowers might be a

wonderful way to express your love and happiness for her if you're a man of few words who wants to show her that you care. The sunflower can be used to represent the soothing and joyful sensation you receive when you look at your partner, whilst the rose is a symbol of love and affection. Additionally, every time your girlfriend sees the flower arrangement in her room, she'll be reminded of your thoughtful gesture.

5. Drive Her Home Late at Night

A long nighttime drive can occasionally be relaxing and romantic. Listening to romantic music while gazing at the endlessly long highways is a terrific way to unwind. Additionally, long drives are a terrific opportunity for in-depth discussions.

6. Give Her Simple But Thoughtful Items

Giving your girlfriend pricey gifts won't necessarily make her happy. Giving her small items that will benefit her in daily life is also a wonderful and kind act. Giving her a pair of warm, comfortable socks or an earbud for when she needs them can mean a lot to her.

7. In public, hold her hand.

Your girlfriend will feel comfortable and protected if you hold her hand in public. Additionally, she will be thrilled to see such a public display of affection and think that you are fortunate to have her.

8. Make her feel special with a weekend getaway

Sometimes taking a little break can make you and your girlfriend more at ease. And what time is better than after a challenging workweek? A weekend excursion to a destination where you two may unwind and enjoy one other's company can be planned.

9. Transmit Her Music

Many people express their love through song. Your sweetheart will be overjoyed if you send her a heartfelt love song. Here is a compilation of wonderful songs in case you need inspiration:

Elvis Presley, "Can't resist falling in love with you"
Elton John, a tiny dancer
You stop me in my tracks, Queen

10. Spend time with her relatives

Her true happiness will come from spending time with her family. Your girlfriend will feel certain that she made the proper choice in choosing you to spend the rest of her life with if you get along with her family.

11. Treat her to a meal at her preferred restaurant

Sometimes, serving your girlfriend's favorite dish from her favorite restaurant will win her heart. Surprise her by bringing her takeout from her preferred restaurant. If you decorate your dining area with candles and play some sultry music in the background, you can also make it a candlelight supper. Her favorite dish in a romantic setting will make your lady very delighted.

12. Text Her Adorable Messages of Love

While sending your girlfriend a simple "I love you" can make her smile, sending something adorable and romantic will make her beam all day long.

To help you get started, consider these texts:

You will always be my lady, my queen, my life, and everything to me, no matter what. I adore you so much!

Since the day you became mine, my life has come into its own; I am so in love with you!

When I'm not with you, a certain area of my heart aches. Realizing this helps me understand how hurt and lost I would be without it.Our hands clung to one another like they were intended for one another.

13. Enjoy Date Nights Out

When you've been dating for a while, date nights are quite crucial. Going on dates may slip both of your minds if you have been dating for a while. But taking your girlfriend out will make her happy and offer you a chance to rediscover that first month of love.

14.Establish Movie Nights

Setting up movie nights is just as vital as regular date nights. After a long day at work, you two may just unwind and enjoy while watching your favorite film. Your girlfriend will feel at ease just by spending time with you in this way.

15. Serve her tea or coffee

Nothing can cheer up your girlfriend more when she needs to get up early and rush to work than finding a cup of freshly brewed coffee or tea made by her favorite person waiting for her.

16. Handle the chores

Every woman in the world, whether they admit it or not, enjoys it when their significant other helps out around the house. Put on those gloves and wash every plate if you really want to make your partner happy.

17. Massage the woman

All your girlfriend would truly want to do is unwind and sleep after a long day of work. You can give her a massage to relieve her stress and sore muscles. She'll experience joy and relaxation as a result at the same time.

18. As often as you can, hug and kiss her

All day long, give your partner lots of hugs and kisses. It makes girls feel special, appreciated, and joyful when their men give them unexpected kisses and hugs.

19. Compose a love letter to her

One of the greatest things you can do for your girlfriend is to write her a love note. She will be thrilled to receive this letter, I'm sure. Express to her your innermost thoughts and how much you miss her when you're apart.

20. Give praise Every female feels valued by her compliments. When you see something positive about your girl, whether it's her smile or

her scent, compliment her frequently. She will be pleased with these praises for sure.

21. Listen To Her Girls appreciate it when men pay attention to them. Whenever she speaks to you, pay attention. When she is discussing a subject she is enthusiastic about or when she is ranting about life in general, pay close attention. While she is speaking, pay her complete attention; she will appreciate it.

22. Consider Her When Making Decisions

Making decisions as a couple is a requirement. Even if you will be the one to make the final decision in your life, involving your girlfriend and giving her opinions some thought will make her feel appreciated and content.

23. Express An Interest In Her Hobbies

You could not enjoy her favorite television shows or films, or you might find her pastimes uninteresting, but that doesn't mean you.By demonstrating enthusiasm while she discusses her favorite program or her interests, you might convince her that you are interested in the things she is passionate about.

24.Share With Her Things

Without holding back, tell her anything, from your sweatshirt to your secrets. This will show her that you want to spend the rest of your lives with her and make her feel special. Being honest and reliable with her will enable her to be equally so with you, which will be advantageous to both of you and your relationship.

25. Remain devoted to her.
Nowadays, it's challenging to locate loyal individuals. Your girlfriend may have encountered her fair share of cheaters in the past. By demonstrating your commitment to her, you could help her feel safe and content. You could accomplish this by expressing your relationship to others or by being more forthcoming with her.

26. Offer Her Your Assistance
You can provide a helping hand to make her life simpler by carrying her luggage, assisting her in locating lost items, or walking her pets. She will be delighted by these unplanned displays of affection and

thankful that she discovered such a wonderful partner.

27. Thank her

When she does anything unique for you, let her know how appreciative you are. A simple "thank you" from you will make her day better and make her feel good about investing more time in the relationship.

28. Treat Her

A female will never turn down being indulged. Whatever she likes, give her chocolates, tiny presents, and other kinds of surprises. To spoil her, you don't have to go overboard or spend a fortune. Little things have a special power.

29. Tell her you love her frequently.

I love you are the three words that are certain to make your girlfriend smile. The entire value of a relationship is contained in these three words. To make her day even more memorable, let her know how you feel about her or surprise her with an unexpected "I love yous." A girl adores it when her lover professes his love for her on a regular basis.

30. Send her romantic notes

Leave her some love notes scribbled on sticky notes. They can be taped on her bathroom mirror, placed in her luggage, or stuck to the refrigerator. She'll be delighted to discover these unexpected love letters from you, and she'll feel valued and special.

Small acts of kindness might make your girlfriend feel your appreciation every day.

A sweet act of kindness, a considerate deed, and taking note of the tiny things she does are all wonderful ways to make your girlfriend smile.

One of the numerous methods to make your girlfriend happy is by sending her a "good morning" message or a quote from one of her favorite novels or movies.

CHAPTER 11;

- Super sexy advice to keep your partner content in bed

It doesn't take a man very long to be very aroused, which is really realistic. However, you cannot generalize the same about women. To get their girlfriend hot and eager for some private time in bed, guys can follow these very simple steps. You must first realize that just because a woman is moist doesn't automatically indicate that she is ready for sex. It could merely be a step toward preparation. Utilizing some of these suggestions can unquestionably ensure that your girlfriend enjoys herself in bed.

- Go at your own pace: Don't jump right in. If you rush things, your wife won't ever feel turned on.

Before the actual act, slow down and indulge in some foreplay. Begin by stroking. Till she is willing for you to reach between her legs, caress her with every inch of her body. Try to discover as much of your partner's physique as you can. Her body can produce delightful feelings in her ears, neck, arms, chest, and legs.

- Find out what she wants: Sometimes, sex should be about your partner. A simple question about what she would like done to her is the finest way to make her feel cherished. You can also ask her about her preferences and things she dislikes. Take this as a chance to find out more about your partner's preferences for bedtime behavior. It lessens the pressure and anxiety for you to try a few things and fail.

-Since kissing doesn't get the respect it merits, a French kiss does not necessarily imply the best kiss. If you didn't know, a lot of ladies don't even like French kissing. Go in slowly, not with an aggressive kiss. Touch her lips gently with yours while you caress hers. Take your time while kissing and let the woman enjoy the sensation of your lips gliding over hers. Kissing shouldn't be a quick act.

- Fondle her properly: Once the two of you have reached a stage where you are ready to advance the relationship, engage in some fondling. Nipples and breasts require a gentle touch because they are so delicate. Don't forget to speak to your women while you chat to them gently and fondle them. Ask her to lead you through the areas where she gets hotter. You can enjoy and tease each other while maintaining communication.

- Give her some time: The goal of touching your woman's body is to get her warmed up and in the mood. You risk losing the fight if you merely push past her legs and grab hold of her. Instead, give her a full body massage before moving on to her private regions while you two are in the mod. Genital play can be made more enjoyable by postponing it somewhat so that your spouse has time to prepare and drip go for you.

- Major Points

For women, emotional connection and closeness are key components of sexual enjoyment.

The true pleasure centers for a woman lie outside of her vagina, therefore foreplay is essential for fulfilling her.

The secret to your partner's sexual fulfillment is to listen to what she wants and take your time to offer her an enjoyable experience.

You must express your passion and desire, but do not go against her wishes.

To improve sex for women, keep in mind that seduction starts in the head and outside of the bedroom.

Everything about love and romantic relationships in all of their guises. By examining people's relationship patterns through the prism of mental health, we try to help individuals love more mindfully and appreciate the wonderful, imperfect love without bias or judgment.

I am your one-stop shop for understanding the enigma of love.

Extra advice for pleasing a woman in bed

And the best advice of all is to let her have her orgasm before you do. She may have to go without an orgasm if you experience one before she does. Improve your erection control, hang in there, and give her the first peak of your passionate encounter. Don't let the fact that she doesn't orgasm during sex make you feel defeated or dissatisfied.

Women rarely orgasm through penetrative intercourse alone, as we have mentioned. Make sure she arrives at the big-O before or after the intercourse to ensure she receives her fair portion of the enjoyment. Take the necessary action, but don't leave her.

www.ingramcontent.com/pod-product-compliance
Lightning Source LLC
LaVergne TN
LVHW010557160826
845677LV00013B/3166

9798848003390